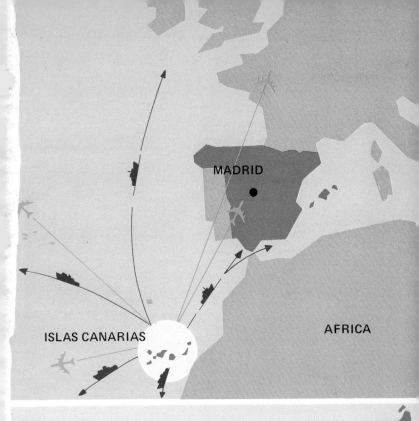

# guide to

# tenerife

AL
MERITO
TURISTICO

MIN. INF. Y TUR.
ESPAÑA

**2nd Edition, February 1988**

I.S.B.N. 84-378-1021-3

Dep. Legal B. 3416-1988

DISTRIBUTOR: ARMANDO PEREZ DIAZ
Amagar, 14 - Tel. 21 67 01-22 06 52
P.O. Box 897
SANTA CRUZ DE TENERIFE (Spain)

# THE GARDEN OF THE HESPERIDES

Legend has it that the Canary Islands are the daughters of King
Atlas: Tenerife, Fuerteventura, Gran Canaria, Lanzarote, Palma,
Gomera and Hierro were said to be the seven descendants of the
mythical monarch. The Islands were mentioned in the works of
Homer, Pindar, and Plato. It was Pliny, however, who gave the Fortunate Islands their first historical names: *Nivaria* and *Canaria.* Some
sources consider that the Canary Islands' name derives from the
Latin word *canis,* referring to the dogs found on the Archipelago by
Juba's expedition, while others state that it comes from *canna* — a
type of reed with poisonous sap. There are also those who believe
that the denomination derived from *Canarii,* the name given to some
tribes who settled on the slopes of Mount Atlas.

The Canary Islands make up an Archipelago lying in the Atlantic
Ocean; because of their beauty the ancients gave them the poetic
name "Garden of the Hesperides." The islands emerge out of the
ocean opposite the coast of Africa and spread over a distance of approximately 300 nautical miles. The Archipelago comprises two major groups of islands, the east and the west. The eastern group,
forming the province of Las Palmas, is made up of Lanzarote,
Fuerteventura, Gran Canaria and the islets of Graciosa, Alegranza,
Montaña Clara, Roque del Oeste, Roque del Este and Lobos (where
the lighthouse is). The western group, comprising Santa Cruz de
Tenerife province, includes the islands of Tenerife, Gomera, La
Palma and Hierro.

The Archipelago is situated between 27° and 29° latitude north and
13° and 18° longitude west. The islands are of volcanic origins; most
of them are characterised by their long and narrow shape, forming
mountainous massifs rising out of the sea. Some, such as Gran

Canaria, are regular in shape, surrounding the crater of an extinct volcano.

The coasts of the islands are almost always rugged; the predominant landscapes are strikingly, originally beautiful. The inland areas, similarly, are characteristically abrupt, which adds a special charm to the views: there are wild mountains and impressive ravines in visual counterpoint to the superb fertile valleys.

The lands in the north of the islands are predominantly green in colour, with extensive banana plantations; whereas the southern areas frequently display solitary desert landscapes where the sun shines brightly almost all the time.

The splendid climate of the Canary Islands constitutes one of their most enchanting features: it is mild, like a practically permanent spring-time — this is naturally one of the Archipelago's many attractions for tourists. The temperature is delightful in summer on the plains and in the coastal areas, attenuated by the sea breezes.

The great abundance of crops is another of the charms of the Canary Islands, not unrelated to the intense development of tourism here. Large quantities of bananas, tobacco and tomatoes are grown: these products, typical of the Canaries, are exported in bulk and constitute a substantial source of income. Other important crops in the Archipelago include sugar-cane, cherimoyas, guavas, kakis and papayas — all characteristic of the islands' lowlands. Citrus fruits, olives, cereals and grapes are also grown, and — in the cooler districts — walnuts, chestnuts, almonds, morello cherries and apples. In this respect special mention should be made of the dragon-tree, which only grows on the Canary Islands. This tree, with a very thick cylindrical bole, belongs to the family of the Liliaceae and is extremely long-lived. Its name derives from the shape of its trunk, similar to a serpent, surmounted by the bristly crest of the tree-top.

**VIEW OF LA LAGUNA.**

The resin known as "dragon blood," which is used as a medicine, is obtained by making incisions in the dragon-tree.

Rain is a very infrequent event on the Archipelago; as a result there are no rivers or streams on the islands, only a few transitory storm torrents. The lands of the Canaries are irrigated by means of the abundant underground reserves of water.

The origins of the Canary Islands are not known with any certainty;

they are, rather, shrouded in a mass of legends. It has been attempted to associate the prehistory of the Archipelago with Atlantis — this theory is based on what Plato wrote concerning the disappearance of the mythical continent under the waters of the ocean. Other writers favour the hypothesis that the Canaries formed part of continental Africa, giving rise to the Archipelago as it is today when they became separated from the mainland.

**VIEW OF TAGANANA.**

The earliest inhabitants of the ancients' "Garden of the Hesperides" were, according to the theory of some historians, Phoenicians. Other sources consider that they were Egyptians; there are also writers who attribute the original settlement of the Archipelago to the Carthaginians, Pelasgians, or Vikings. In fact there are all kinds of theories in this regard, but no certain scientific evidence supporting any of them. According to the most reliable researches carried out, it seems that the first inhabitants of the Canary Islands belonged to three different groups: the Guanches, Semites and Hamites. This original population had a very primitive way of life, which only evolved very slowly. The majority lived in natural caves — which exist to this day — and grew wheat and barley. Their basic foodstuff was *gofio* (ground, roast cereals), still one of the typical dishes of the Islands. They also ate meat from dogs, pigs and sheep, seafood that they caught off the coasts, and butter and cheese made from goats' milk.

The Guanches stored animal fat in wooden receptacles and used it to mummify their dead. It seems that after washing the corpse, they exposed it to the effects of the open air and sunlight. Once the body was dry, they covered it with fat and various aromatic herbs; and then placed it in some out-of-the way cave. Just like the ancient Egyptians, they left food and diverse utensils by the side of the bodies, so as to facilitate their life after death.

The Guanches were proficient in the production of bone spears, fishhooks, burins, axes and other tools. Although they had no writing, characters carved on stones by the Guanches have been found in some places on the islands. The structure of these signs is similar to that of certain cave paintings.

The Guanche society was organised on a strictly patriarchal basis and divided into three hierarchical groups: the royal family, the

nobility, and the common people. This primitive society attached great importance, in the religious field, to the priests called *faicanes* and the *harimaguadas* or sacred virgins. The latter in practice lost their nature as such, at least in relation to the king, for it seems that he exercised a kind of droit du seigneur over them.


# HISTORICAL OUTLINE OF THE ISLANDS

It was the Romans who, on arriving on the Canary Islands, gave the Archipelago the name "Fortunate Islands." Later, in the Middle Ages, the Arabs called the Canaries *Kaledat.* Giovanni Boccaccio da Certaldo was one of the first Europeans to write about the Archipelago. The Vivaldi brothers, from Genoa, set sail for the "Fortunate Islands" in the late 13th century, but it is not known whether they actually disembarked there. Later, at the beginning of the 14th century, another Genoese — Lancelotto Malocello — succeeded in reaching the Canaries and settled on one of the islands, which he gave the name Lanzarote. In the course of the same century, expeditions from the Balearic Islands, Catalonia and Portugal arrived at the Archipelago. An expedition made up of Andalusians and Basques reached the Canary Islands at the end of the 14th century, returning to the Peninsula with a considerable number of native prisoners and varied, abundant booty.

The Frenchman Jean de Béthencourt was, however, the first to settle on the Canary Islands for a substantial period of time, after succeeding in conquering a number of them. Béthencourt apparently disembarked on the Archipelago around the year 1402. Once he had

**SNOW AND CLOUDS WELCOME US IN THE NEIGHBOURHOOD OF EL TEIDE.**

consolidated a relatively firm position on part of the Canaries, he travelled to Spain and obtained the title of King of the Canary Islands from Henry III of Castile. Béthencourt successfully concluded the conquest of Lanzarote, Fuerteventura and Hierro, but suffered a severe defeat when he tried to capture Gran Canaria: he decided to withdraw from the Islands and returned to France definitively in 1405.

The islands conquered by Béthencourt (he never succeeded in taking Tenerife, Gran Canaria or La Palma, which remained independent) later became the property of various different personages. One of them, Diego de Herrera, sold his rights over the conquered islands to the Catholic Monarchs Ferdinand and Isabella, who then decided to undertake the conquest of the whole Archipelago.

The historical figures associated with the Canary Islands include Luis de la Cerda, a descendant of S Louis, King of France. Oddly enough, de la Cerda never set foot on the Islands; his connection with the history of the "Garden of the Hesperides" was a result of Pope Clement VI's decision to grant him the title of Prince of La Fortuna, in 1344. This appointment accredited him as lord of the Canary Islands: his dominions included Canaria, Nigaria, Pluviaria, Capraria, Juniona, Embronea, Atlantis, Hesperide, Gorgona and Cernent. This sovereignty was more fantastic than real; nine of the aforementioned islands were in theory located in the middle of the Atlantic.

In the course of the 16th century the Archipelago was the scene of numerous violent feats of arms protagonised by a variety of pirates and corsairs. An important skirmish occurred in 1522, when Juan Florín seized Moctezuma's treasure which Hernán Cortés had sent to Charles I of Spain (Charles V of Germany): this was one of the earliest, and bloodiest, battles conducted in the Canary Islands. They

were later attacked on many different occasions: the most significant incursions were led by Saintonge, Calafat, Jean Capdeville, Menjouyn de la Cabanne, Van der Doez, Blake, and Nelson.

In the 18th century Las Palmas (Gran Canaria) and La Laguna (Tenerife) competed for the status of capital of the Archipelago, although there were a corregidor, council and magistrate on each island.

After these eventful centuries, the "Fortunate Islands" lived up to their name in the 19th, when they enjoyed a period of calm and prosperity. An event that was to prove decisive for the future of the Canary Islands occurred at the middle of last century: on July 11th 1852 Queen Isabella II converted the ports of the Archipelago into free ports. This step was to cause a progressive increase in the development of marine commerce and the local economy, first, and then — at the height of the 20th century — to contribute decisively to the tourist boom that has had such a positive effect on the islands' prosperity in recent years.

EL TEIDE ETCHED OUT AGAINST THE SKY BEHIND THIS LANDSCAPE OF THE NORTH COAST.

THE PLAZA DE ESPAÑA OPENS GENEROUSLY TO THE FRESH SEA BREEZES.

# TENERIFE

The island of the white mountain — snowy Teide, whose silhouette is visible from the sea and which, with an altitude of some 3,716 metres above sea-level, is the highest peak in the Spanish nation — is roughly triangular in shape. It lies in the centre of the Archipelago and measures 81 km long by 45 km wide. Tenerife's littoral is irregular and rugged, with splendid bays and sheltered harbours, the most outstanding being at Santa Cruz, the capital city of the island. Miguel de Unamuno left us a superb, profound description of the island: "And there in the distance, above the stern towering crests and the rugged black rocks, above the sea — no longer of water, but of mist — stood the island of Tenerife, like a celestial vision, dominated by that gigantic watchtower of Spain, the peak of Teide. The sight of this immense throne rising out of the clouds really seemed to distance me from the narrow confines where I was walking. One would have said that the island was suspended in the sky, for a sea of mist covered and overwhelmed the ocean of water. One's sight rested on that vision, as if on something lacking material tangibility, something that had appeared merely to delight one's eyes and captivate one's heart."

One of the ancient legends of the original inhabitants of Tenerife stated that gigantic birds with white wings would arrive by sea and subjugate the lords of the islands. Another of Tenerife's legends — versions of which also exist on other islands in the Archipelago — refers to the existence of Malpaís ('Bad Country'), an extensive desert where no flowers or banana-plants grow, and where no birds fly. Malpaís is a silent land: there are no villages, no shepherds, no

flocks; nor are there trees. It is a land where silence and solitude reign, like premonitions of death. The islanders speak of Malpaís with mysterious awe, as if it had really existed. The legendary existence of Malpaís would explain the mystery concerning explorers who were never able to supply information about the island, although they had disembarked on it: they would seem to have fled hastily, terrified....

Tenerife is the largest island in the Archipelago; the three headlands delimiting it are Punta Anaga, Punta de Teno and Punta de Rasca. The island's landscapes display dazzling contrasts: in some areas Nature is gentle, docile in appearance, while in others the ruggedness of the views is simultaneously imposing and attractive.

The outstanding landmarks of Tenerife's history include the arrival of the squadron led by Fernando de Ormel in 1386; the disembarkation of Alonso Fernández de Lugo at Puerto de Añaza, coming from Gran Canaria (he was to lay the foundations of Santa Cruz); the incursions of pirates throughout the 16th century; the island's defence against Nelson's squadron in 1797, in which the famous English admiral was defeated and lost an arm.... In the 19th century Tenerife enjoyed a period of prosperity (common to the whole Archipelago), the starting-point of the dynamic development characterising the Islands in the present century.

Among the most remarkable of the illustrious natives of Tenerife were José de Anchieta, the apostle of Brazil (16C); the poet Antonio de Viana, who was a friend of Lope de Vega; Juan Núñez de la Peña, the royal chronicler (17C); Guillén del Castillo, who took part in the conquest of the Philippines; Leopoldo O'Donnell, a leading political figure in 19th-century Spain; Juan Bautista Bérriz; Juan Bautista

Antequera, who was Navy Minister and travelled round the world on board the ''Numancia''; and the musician Teobaldo Power.

In the words of Armas Marcelo, the writer from the Canaries, ''The most profound, intimate idiosyncrasy of today's inhabitants of Tenerife could be summed up in the concept of *chicharrerismo.* The term *chicharrero,* in its origins unequivocally pejorative and specific, was applied exclusively to the inhabitants of Santa Cruz de Tenerife

by those from other parts of the island, especially La Laguna: the intention was to confirm outright the traditional dissension by humiliating the inhabitants of a city of little class, lineage or history, whose industrial and economic possibilities were limited to catching, selling and consuming the lowly fish known as *chicharro* (horse mackerel). Nowadays, however, the term is brandished with pride by the inhabitants of almost the whole island, as a label vindicating their particular characteristics, to the point that a monument to the *Chicharro* stands proudly in one of the most central spots in the capital city.''

## CLIMATE AND FLORA

The island of Tenerife enjoys an ideal climate. The mean temperature oscillates around 20° C. Together with the beauty of the island's landscapes and the abundance of excellent beaches, this has had a decisive influence on the extraordinary influx of tourists to Tenerife. The lands of Tenerife benefit from the effects of the trade winds, bringing humidity from the Atlantic: this circumstance prevents the climate from being excessively dry and has a positive influence on the growth of the island's splendid flora.

Agriculture plays a very important rôle as a source of income for the island. Among the principal crops, mention should be made of *papas,* potatoes, which are grown in both dry and irrigated areas: three harvests are obtained each year on Tenerife. Arona, Arico, Güimar and San Miguel are the leading districts as regards the production of potatoes. English varieties are generally used for the first crop; the seeds from previous crops are used for the rest of the year, until seeds are imported from England again for the following year.

THE STEEP RUGGED COASTLINE NEAR ALMÁCIGA.

Bananas are another of the most important crops. Banana plantations cover the valley of La Orotava, Los Realejos and the district
around Puerto de la Cruz.

Considerable amounts of tomatoes are also grown, principally in the
lands of La Laguna, Adeje and Güimar.

Tobacco is another important crop: Tenerife is the leading island in
the Archipelago as regards its production, in the same way as it is the
main producer of Canary wines. Sugar-cane is grown in the lands of
Valle Guerra, El Rosario and Tejina.

Many almond-trees blossom around Guía de Isora. Other outstanding crops on Tenerife include vegetables, cereals, onions, maize and
fruit. There are many fields of barley, rye and maize in the unirrigated
intermediate and upper lands facing south and north-west.

The island is divided into three clearly differentiated zones as regards
its luxuriant vegetation: the areas between Taganana and Bufadero,
La Victoria de Acentejo and Candelaria, and San Juan de la Rambla
and Vilaflor, including the Teide district. On the Anaga peninsula,
within the first-mentioned zone, there are many dragon-trees, while
potatoes, grapes and tomatoes are grown; five hundred yards away
these crops are replaced by laurel, holly and beech-trees, which are
succeeded — from La Cruz de Taganana onwards — by
undergrowth and heather. The cliffs of the north begin in the second
zone, where there are prickly pears and potatoes, tomatoes, maize
and vines are cultivated; as the land gets higher, heather, holly and
pine-trees appear. From San Juan de la Rambla up to an altitude of
some 1,000 metres, the predominant crops are bananas, tomatoes,
vines, maize, potatoes and chestnuts; there are also palm-trees.
Above the height of 1,000 metres grow heather, holly, beech-trees,
gorse and pines, which fade out towards Telde. On the slopes on the
other side of the mountain, towards Vilaflor, vineyards make their

appearance once again, and also fields of cereals, potatoes, tomatoes and almond-trees.

From the early 16th century onwards, once the conquest of the Archipelago had been completed, the cultivation of sugar-cane was one of the islands' main sources of income. The following century, however, this crop went into decline and was replaced by Peruvian potatoes and maize brought from Mexico.

The dragon-tree is a very characteristic sight in the landscapes of Tenerife; this tree only grows in the Canary Islands. The sap of the dragon-tree was praised by mediaeval poets and its medicinal properties were used in very early times. It seems that the magicians of the Middle Ages used it to cure the plague of leprosy. Dante was impressed by the existence of this tree because it "perspired" blood. One can see dragon-trees nowadays in the districts of Los Realejos, La Laguna and Icod.

The fact that a liquid similar to blood flows from the dragon-tree's bark if one makes an incision in it led the natives to consider it as a kind of fabulous animal from another world, a world where all fantasies are possible. Luis Diego Cuscoy wrote that the dragon-tree "is a miracle of vegetation allowing us to view alive, fresh and leafy something that elsewhere is death, remains, fossils." The existence of this fabulous tree on the Canaries has given rise to hypotheses according to which the islands must have been in contact with the lands of the Mediterranean, and shared a common geography with them, up to the late Tertiary period.

Mention should be made of another colourful element in the distinctive landscapes of the Canary Islands: the existence of charming birds, in particular — par excellence — canaries, such admirable

**BAJAMAR STANDS IN ONE OF THE MOST POPULAR TOURIST SPOTS.**

singing birds. It seems that there was a great variety of species of birds on the Archipelago in former times, especially turtle-doves, rock pigeons, blackbirds and falcons. There was still an abundance of birds on the islands in the 19th century; it was gradually reduced as a result of the continuous, indiscriminate felling of woodlands. Falcons were particularly numerous on Tenerife until the beginning of the 17th century; and there were abundant finches, with superb plumage, until the 19th. There are still many wild canaries nowadays.

## FOLK CULTURE

The folk culture of the Canary Islands has been determined by three main factors: the heritage of the Guanches, the conquistadores' influence on the Archipelago, and diverse contributions from Spanish America. The typical music and songs of the Canaries are characterised by a melodious cadence common to all the islands in the Archipelago, which gives them a markedly distinctive nature. These local features have been conserved with an extraordinary degree of purity; their foundations survive to this day, shaping the particularly Canary personality of the authochthonous songs and dances. The most outstanding include the *tajaraste,* the *tanganillo,* the *Santo Domingo* and the *saltones.* In other manifestations of the islands' folklore, such as the *tango,* the *jota,* and the *malagueña,* it is easy to recognise influences from Spain or America.

The peculiarities of the Canary Islanders' way of life are clearly reflected in the *isas* and the *folías.* The latter dance, distinguished by its slowness and gentleness, is typical of Tenerife, while the *isas* — with a livelier rhythm — correspond to Gran Canaria.

◁ ALMÁCIGA AND NEARBY COAST.

SPECIMEN OF THE GIANT CACTUS, ABUNDANT IN THE ISLAND.

THE ELEGANCE OF THE ORCHID IS A PERFECT REFLECTION OF THE ▷
SPIRIT OF THE ISLAND.

Cradle songs are also very deeply-rooted in the Archipelago: these compositions are characterised by their simplicity of form, causing the inhabitants to relive sensations evoking their childhood dreams and accentuating their sentimentalism. The same is true of the charming Christmas carols, which are played in the streets by the *Divinos,* typical bands of street musicians whose members wear attractively colourful costumes.

The *timple,* a kind of small guitar similar to the ukulele, is the musical instrument of the Canary Islands par excellence: a genuinely Canary instrument which is not found anywhere else but in the Archipelago of the "Fortunate Islands."

White is the predominant colour in both the men's and women's typical apparel. The Canary woman's costume is generally made up of a long dress with coloured stripes, a black woollen jerkin over a white bodice, a silk scarf tied around the neck and a yellow-coloured mantilla with trimmings of ribbon, or else a small black hat with a scarf tied at the back of the neck. Straw hats, with ribbons and flowers, are also highly typical.

The men's costume comprises white trousers, gaiters, a white shirt, a black or coloured waistcoat, and a wide-brimmed hat hanging on the back. The male inhabitants often bear a long stick in the right hand. The most typically Canary costume, that of the *mago,* is now only worn in pilgrimages and local festivities (the term *mago* derives from the name given to the country people of the Archipelago, in particular those who keep flocks or work the land).

The principal festivities held on Tenerife feature a traditional, bucolic atmosphere. The Latins' classicism was introduced into the Archipelago by the conquistadores; the islands' celebrations still emphasise the ritual aspect of the cultivation and harvest of cereals. On these occasions, floral arches and hearts symbolise the triumph of

mankind over Nature, and also the inhabitants' gratitude to the land that provides their sustenance.

The *fiestas* commemorating the Cross and the foundation of Santa Cruz de Tenerife, the capital city, are held from the 1st to the 10th of May. The festivity celebrated in the capital, on July 25th, to commemorate the victory over the squadron led by Horatio Nelson is another important event. On the first Sunday in June La Laguna celebrates *fiestas* in honour of San Antonio Abad (S Antony); this festivity features a highly characteristic atmosphere of folklore and has become very popular. Other important celebrations include those held at Puerto de la Cruz in honour of the 'Virgen del Carmen' in the second fortnight of June; the Octave of Corpus Christi and the pilgrimage of S Isidore at La Orotava; the 'Santísimo Cristo' *fiesta* at La Laguna, on September 14th; and the festivities of Our Lady of Candlemas, on August 14th, in the course of which a pastoral re-enactment of the appearance of this image to the Guanches is carried out. Legend has it that the image of Our Lady of Candlemas was found at Chirigai beach by a group of Guanches at the end of the 14th century.

The *romerías* — popular pilgrimages — held on the island are characterised by their fascinating local colour and accompanied by processions, music, singing and dances. The people's fervour is particularly intense on the occasion of the famous entry of the figure of Christ into La Laguna, which is accompanied by a great show of fireworks.

## SPORTS

Special mention should be made of the very ancient sport called

"Canary wrestling," which really forms a part of the Archipelago's great heritage of folk culture. This is a highly manly activity, conducted in conformity with strictly gentlemanly rules. The strength and skill of the competitors play a fundamental rôle in the practice of this genuinely Canary sport.

Another traditional sport — although its practice seems to be gradually diminishing — is the *juego de palo* ("stick game"), in the course of which the competitors defend themselves and strike one another with long staffs. This activity apparently goes back to the time when the Guanches lived in independence on the Archipelago. The popularity of cockfights was quite firmly established on the Canaries in times gone by; nowadays, however, these combats — introduced into the islands by Spanish Americans — are practically never organised.

Over and above these traditionally Canary sports, many others are practised in the Archipelago. There is an extensive following for football in Tenerife, which has always featured first-class teams and constituted a breeding ground producing major figures of Spanish football. There are also a large number of devotees of boxing, hunting and fishing; golf, tennis, pelota, skating, pigeon shooting, horseriding and swimming are practised too. Angling and underwater fishing have become increasingly popular in Tenerife in recent times.

## CRAFT WORK

The needlework pieces elaborated by the women of Tenerife occupy an outstanding place among the island's typical craft work. It would be no exaggeration to say that there is not a single village in Tenerife

where openwork and embroidery are not practised, although Puerto de la Cruz, Los Realejos and La Orotava are the towns enjoying the greatest prestige in this respect. There are still some elderly women who spin on their old, rustic looms at Tegueste and Taganana. The articles created by the women of Tenerife attract one's attention by virtue of their characteristically exquisite taste. They are made with infinite patience and reproduce extraordinarily bright, fascinatingly colourful landscapes. Particular mention should also be made of the craft textiles woven of wool or flax. All these typical products of Tenerife offer not only the attraction of good craftsmanship, but also the charm of knowing that this is a phenomenon that is disappearing, is no longer easy to find.

Another very interesting field within the world of Tenerife's craft work is that of ceramics. Some old Guanche potteries survive to this day; the ceramic pieces are reddish in colour and the naive roughness of their shapes is particularly attractive.

Other articles typical of Tenerife's craft work include the carved wooden utensils and the knives with beautiful enamelled hilts used in the banana plantations. Special mention should be made of the island's production of basketwork pieces: the baskets made of reeds and wickerwork are particularly charming, as are the straw hats. The inhabitants work palm leaves, reeds, rushes and wicker with extraordinary skill, thus creating baskets, brushes, hats and other objects.

## CUISINE

The Archipelago of the Canary Islands features a very distinctive style of cooking: It is substantially different from the cuisines of the rest of Spain, and offers an extensive variety of typical dishes.

*Gofio,* the ancient Guanches' dish, remained one of the basic elements in the diet of the islands' country people after the Con-

quest. It is made of ground, roast cereals, and they eat it with coffee and milk for breakfast and combined with bananas, fish and soup at their midday and evening meals.

The cuisine of the Archipelago includes such delicious dishes as *puchero canario* ('Canary stew'), made with the classic "seven meats": pork, ox meat, beef, rabbit, partridge, pigeon and chicken. This is obviously a very substantial dish, which should be consumed at leisure and accompanied by a good wine from Tenerife.

*Mojo picón* or *mojo colorado* — or simply *mojo* — is another typical dish of the Canary Islands, based on a highly seasoned sauce made with oil, garlic, vinegar, cumin seeds, red peppers, paprika and salt. The paprika can be replaced by parsley, in which case the sauce is known as *mojo verde.*

Another dish with a great tradition on the Archipelago is *sancocho,* elaborated with potatoes, *mojo picón, gofio* and boiled fish.

Further dishes of Canary cuisine include *papas arrugadas* (potatoes) accompanied by *mojo picón (viejas,* a variety of fish highly esteemed by the islanders, can also be added); boiled dogfish in a sauce, or roasted; Tenerife casserole; fried kid *a la portuense;* horse mackerel; sweet sausages; *tasarte asado;* stuffed horse mackerel; *javeadas;* and *fragollo* (crushed and boiled corn). The tomatoes of the Canary Islands, which are of high quality, are used to complement no few typical dishes of the islands' cuisine.

As regards desserts, mention should be made in the first place of the bananas and other delicious fruits that abound in the Archipelago; one should then cite the *turrón* (a kind of nougat) made from *gofio, alegrías* (nougat with sesame), *rapaduras* (based on *gofio* and molasses), the Christmas sweets elaborated at La Laguna and Puerto de la Cruz, the white cheeses made according to craft tradition in the south of Tenerife, almond cheese, cheesecake from Hierro, and *bienmesabe.*

ALL THE EXAMPLES OF THE ISLAND FLORA ARE MAGNIFICENTLY COLOURED. ▷

EL TEIDE AND THE RICH VEGETATION ARE BOTH INTEGRAL PARTS OF LA OROTAVA.

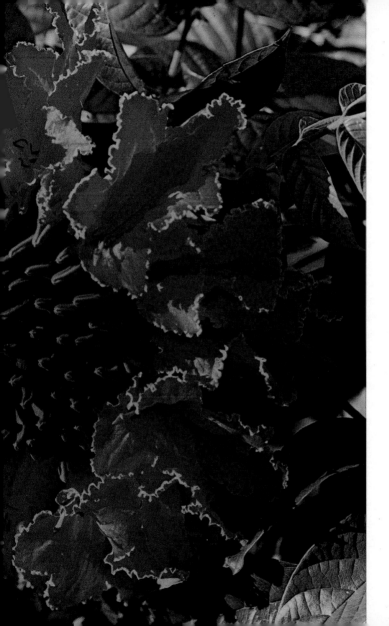

A great deal of wine was produced on the islands in the 18th century, and the vintages from the Canaries were justly famous. The production declined later on, but there are still some excellent wines elaborated on Tenerife, Lanzarote and Gran Canaria. The red and white wines of these islands are very suitable for accompanying the typically Canary dishes. The muscatels, recommended with desserts, are also of great quality. Two other drinks should be mentioned: the fine, traditional malvasia (malmsey) and Canary rum, which the islanders dilute with honey.

## TYPICAL CANARY ARCHITECTURE

Although there is no specifically differentiated type of house typical of the Canary Islands, the dwellings generally display a number of characteristics configurating a distinctive design. In general, the old houses have spacious interior courtyards surrounded by galleries of teak-wood and adorned with many pots containing flowers and plants. Other typically Canary elements include broad eaves and large balconies of carved wood, which project from the houses' façades and usually have enchanting wooden shutters.

The most modest houses feature a single storey, of masonry or concrete, with the roof thatched with straw. In the working people's houses on the coastline there is a terrace in place of the roof.

One of the distinctive features of the Canary people's dwellings is their cleanness and the exquisite way in which they are decorated, with a profusion of flowers and plants of the most diverse species. In some areas there are still picturesque caves fitted out as houses: the interior is always immaculately clean and lovingly adorned.

# THE CAPITAL OF TENERIFE

Santa Cruz de Tenerife, the capital of the island of Tenerife and of the province of the same name, is located on a plain delimited by the Anaga mountain range to the north. It stands by a magnificent bay and has a splendid seaport, of great importance in trade and tourism, where the principal Spanish and international shipping lines put in. Santa Cruz is also served by a large airport, Los Rodeos, some 13 km from the centre of the city.

The capital city of Tenerife enjoys an exceptionally mild climate: the minimum temperature is never less than 10° C. The summers are not excessively hot, even in July and August. Rainfall is scarce; the highest measurements generally correspond to the month of April. On most days the sky is enchantingly blue, with no clouds.

# THE BEACHES OF TENERIFE

The magnificent sands of Las Teresitas, with an extension of some 1.2 km, lie at a distance of 10 kilometres from the capital of Tenerife. Other very popular beaches include El Arenal, half a kilometre long, located at Bajamar, 23 km away from the capital; and that of Martiánez, about 400 m long, at Puerto de la Cruz, some 42 km from Santa Cruz. There are many other beaches on the island; the most remarkable are San Marcos beach, at Icod, 66 km away from the capital of the island, which stretches over about 250 m; and El Médano beach, 1.5 km long, 93 km from Santa Cruz.

All these beaches are practically invaded by bathers almost all the year round, with large numbers of tourists flocking from the Spanish Peninsula and various foreign countries.

DETAIL OF PUERTO DE LA CRUZ.

## THE HARBOUR

Although fewer visitors to the island arrive by sea each year, Santa Cruz de Tenerife harbour is still one of the vital, central parts of the city. The site where the silhouette of San Cristóbal castle used to stand (this military fortress, together with the nearby castle of San Juan — built in the 18th century — served to defend the harbour) is now occupied by the Plaza de España, the entrance to the harbour area. Two large statues of warriors dominate the extension of the square, which is flanked by the buildings accommodating the installations of the 'Cabildo Insular' (Island Council) and the Post Office. The Archaeological Museum, in the same building as the Island Council, contains an important collection of prehistoric Guanche objects.

DETAIL OF PUERTO DE LA CRUZ FROM LAKE MARTIÁNEZ.

The terraces of two bars here — the "Atlántico" and the "Kiosco Alameda," popularly known as "Los Paragüitas" — are the meeting-place for a clientèle principally made up of natives of Santa Cruz. Plaza de España is a strategical point from which to observe the life of the city.

## THE CITY

The first settlement to exist at Santa Cruz de Tenerife grew up around Barrio del Cabo. This was originally a small group of huts, and became a village as such around the year 1500; the next quarters to be established were La Caleta, El Barranquillo and Plaza de la Iglesia. The essential structure of the city that was to become the capital of the island was defined by the end of the 16th century; Guanches and conquistadores lived side by side in the township. Calle del Castillo, Calle de la Candelaria and Calle de la Cruz Verde date from this period. Not until the 18th century, however, was Santa Cruz de Tenerife to be consolidated as a major city, in which the commercial activity of the harbour was to play a key rôle. The architectural school known as the "Canary colonial style," which left fine specimens in Santa Cruz, was also born in the Age of Enlightenment (18th century).

Traces of the capital city's history are to be found in the streets near the lower part of the Barranco de Santos; Fernández de Lugo's expedition disembarked very near here, on the beaches of Añaza, in 1493. This was also where the Cross (Cruz) of the Conquest, the origin of Santa Cruz de Tenerife, was raised.

**TWO VIEWS OF THE MAGNIFICENT HOTEL INSTALLATIONS.**

Behind the interesting church of Nuestra Señora de la Concepción, one can visit one of the most evocative corners in the city, Plaza de la Iglesia, with a palm-tree and a cross in the centre of the square. The whitewashed façades of the houses around this square impregnate it with a characteristically Canary atmosphere. Casa de Fusé is the most outstanding building, with its beautiful wooden balcony and architecture typical of the Archipelago.

To the north of Plaza de la Iglesia is Plaza de la Isla de la Madera, where the city's old market — La Recova Vieja — used to be located. The Municipal Theatre, inaugurated in 1851, occupies a whole block here: it stands on the former site of a Dominican monastery which played a brilliant rôle in the defence of the city against the squadron led by Nelson in 1797. The theatre was later given the name of Angel Guimerá, the great playwright from the Canary Islands who settled in Barcelona and became one of the most popular figures of the Catalan theatre.

The shopping area of the city has grown up around Plaza de la Candelaria. In the centre of this rectangular square stands an obelisk surmounted by a statue of Our Lady of Candlemas. Plaza de España is the next square, surrounded by important commercial establishments. The two most characteristic buildings are the 'Casino Principal' and the 'Palacio de Carta,' the former seat of the Government House, now accommodating a bank. There is a proliferation of traders, the majority Hindus, in this area, with many shops selling imported goods, especially cameras, cine cameras, tape recorders, radios, watches, transistors....

Calle del Castillo (the name derives from San Cristóbal castle) is an extension of the shopping area. There are numerous shops in this street, both long-established concerns and modern boutiques. Calle de Imeldo Serís, popularly known as Calle del Barranquillo, runs

parallel to Calle del Castillo: this is a narrow street, crowded with heterogeneous shops.

The commercial life of the city also extends on the other side of Plaza de la Candelaria, along Calle de Bethencourt Alfonso (also known as Calle de San José) and Calle de Villalba Hervás; Plaza del Príncipe, boasting superb laurel-trees, is at the end of these streets. This square was the centre of the city's social life in the first third of the 20th century; its appearance is somewhat decadent nowadays, with 19th-century statues and stone parapets. The Municipal Band performs on the bandstand in the centre every Sunday, playing more or less classical compositions. The walls of the old Franciscan monastery of S Peter of Alcántara stand opposite the square.

By taking Calle del Castillo the visitor can reach Plaza de Weyler, which is quadrilateral in shape, with well-tended gardens and flowerbeds and a fountain in the middle. This spacious square is flooded with light and gaiety. The Military Headquarters of the Canary Islands stands by the square; the old building of the Military Hospital is in the vicinity, on the edge of the ravine by Puente (Bridge) Galcerán.

Plaza de Weyler is a centre of considerable activity in the life of the city. The bus station from which the *guaguas* connected the capital with different villages on the island was located in the nearby Plaza del Hospital Militar until recently. Although the bus station is now in Calle de Imeldo Serís, near Plaza de España, Plaza de Weyler is still the meeting-place for the numerous Canary country people who come to the capital: groups of people form here every morning to speculate with the shares of the companies which exploit the resources of water that spring from underground galleries and are used for the irrigation of the whole of Tenerife.

Various streets lead out from Plaza de Weyler: one of the most important is Calle de Méndez Núñez, which extends as far as the

Ramblas. This is a long street in which a number of public buildings stand, such as the Gobierno Civil (Government House), the Ayuntamiento (City Hall) and the Instituto Nacional de Previsión (National Health Service).

Half-way along Calle de Méndez Núñez, on the left-hand side, is one of the longest sides of García Sanabria Municipal Park, which is located on a vast terrace surmounted by a large floral clock. The other sides of the Park give onto the Ramblas, Calle de Numancia, and Calle del Doctor Naveiras (popularly known as Los Campos). In the geometrical centre of the Municipal Park, where all its avenues converge, there is a fine pool stocked with swans and ducks. A number of remarkable sculptures by Pablo Serrano, Claude Viseux, Guinovart and other well-known artists were installed in the Municipal Park on the occasion of the 1st International Exhibition of Sculpture in the Street, organised in this setting in 1973: these works adorn the Park to this day.

The avenue known as Las Ramblas crosses the city diagonally from one side to the other; it is made up of the boulevards called Avenida de los Reyes Católicos, Avenida de la Asunción, and Avenida del General Franco. The three boulevards constitute a single avenue with a broad, beautiful walk for pedestrians in the centre, flanked by benches and trees, with tasteful street-lamps at regular intervals. There is an original sculpture by Xavier Corberó in the space between Calle de Ramos Serrano and Calle de Robayna.

The "Acidalio Lorenzo" municipal swimming-pool is at the beginning of the Avenida de los Reyes Católicos. After passing the Avenida de la Asunción, the visitor will reach Plaza de la Paz, the

TWO VIEWS OF LAKE MARTIÁNEZ.

nerve-centre of the Ramblas, full of animation from dawn to dusk. A number of cinemas and cafés stand in this square. The Bull-Ring is located a little further along the avenue.

The Ramblas become more and more beautiful as one continues along the popular avenue towards the sea. It is flanked by fascinating buildings displaying architecture typical of the Canary Islands, and also by gardens. The Hotel Mencey is in this area: this establishment is always full of foreign tourists from the furthest corners of the world, and of members of Tenerife's high society.

The corner of the Ramblas and Calle de Méndez Núñez has a very distinctive ambience. There are several bars and restaurants in the vicinity: this is an eminently gastronomical quarter. Establishments such as La Riviera, La Estancia, La Masía II, La Bella Napoli, Dorada, Hong-Kong, Sacho, La Fontana de Oro and many others in this area serve all the gastronomical specialities of the Canaries and dishes drawn from the varied cuisine of the Spanish Peninsula and the rest of the world.

The side wall of Almeida barracks stands parallel to the Ramblas, towards the end of the avenue. The handsome boulevard ends in Avenida de Anaga, which, continued by various roads, leads north-west into the interior of the island.

El Toscal quarter — situated more or less between Avenida de Anaga, Calle de Méndez Núñez, Calle de San Isidro and Plaza del Príncipe — is a labyrinth of narrow, winding streets and alleys, generally lined with old one-storey houses. This is a working people's quarter still retaining some of the old *ciudadelas,* tenement buildings with small rooms grouped around a communal patio.

El Toscal quarter, in the very centre of Tenerife's capital city, displays a popular image — both architecturally and socially — com-

plemented by fascinating, enchanting human aspects. A kind of cant, very difficult to understand, characterised by its peculiar expressions and indolently pronounced apocopes, is even spoken in this quarter. This way of speaking is called *nota* or *mata.* Armas Marcelo wrote that "*Mata,* or *matiento,* has been part of the traditions of Santa Cruz practically since time immemorial (...) The curious aspect is that this way of speaking was soon used, in imitation, as another of the signs of identity that some groups of society wished to vindicate as proof of their *chicharrerismo:* they thus helped to make this culture universal and to convert El Toscal into the cradle, and bastion, of the profoundest values of this city, a place where the quotidian is still revered and its most picturesque aspects are affectionately highlighted."

Armas Marcelo added that "One could say that the main entrance (to El Toscal quarter) is in Plaza del Patriotismo, next to Plaza del Príncipe, from whence leads Calle de La Rosa — the main street in all the area and, as a result, the least idiosyncratic. This street divides the quarter into an upper and a lower area; in relation to its course one can still define certain differences as regards the occupations of El Toscal's original inhabitants: in this way, it is possible to observe that as one approaches the sea, workshops and establishments related to it in one way or another begin to appear, to the point that Calle de la Marina (which, as its name — 'Navy Street' — indicates, leads to the quays) is the main base for customs agents and shipping brokers."

In Calle de San José those fond of night life will find busy discotheques, bingo parlours and other establishments that do not close until the early hours of the morning. There are many singles bars and night clubs in this area.

There are also various private clubs in the capital city of Tenerife, some of them of a popular nature, such as the Recreo in Calle Ruiz

de Padrón, others more select, for example the Casino Principal in Plaza de la Candelaria or the Real Club Náutico (Royal Yacht Club). The most outstanding of the more recently established centres is the Club Oliver, which offers modern installations, distinguished gardens and an excellent swimming-pool.

Other establishments frequented by devotees of night life include the Shanghai Bar (Calle de la Marina), Orche (Calle de Méndez Núñez), the O'Clock (Pasaje Sitjá), El Aguila (Calle de San José) and El Monitor (Calle de Numancia).

Some of the most highly reputed restaurants in the city are La Caseta de Madera, which has the keel of a boat in place of the counter (located at the end of the Avenida Marítima); Mesón Tagoro (Plaza del Patriotismo); El Puntero, in the city centre; Las Cuevas (this establishment is carved out of the rock, in Avenida de Anaga); Dong-Kinh, a Vietnamese restaurant (Calle 25 de Julio); Mesón Castellano (Calle de Lima); and Cueva Caprichosa, a picturesque restaurant installed in a natural cave, splendidly decorated, where one can eat excellent meat dishes, some 7 km away from Santa Cruz — not far from the Taco quarter.

◁ THE EXUBERANT GARDENS OF ICOD DE LOS VINOS.

# CHURCH OF NUESTRA SEÑORA DE LA CONCEPCION

'The Conception of Our Lady' is the oldest parish in Santa Cruz de Tenerife; the present-day church was built, on the ruins of the one raised in the time of Adelantado (Governor) Fernández de Lugo, in the mid-17th century. The original church had been destroyed by a

THE AGE-OLD DRAGON TREE OF ICOD DE LOS VINOS.

fire in the year 1652. The interesting sights preserved in the interior include two excellent carvings — a *Madonna* and a *S Joseph* — by Luján Pérez, the famous 18th-century maker of religious images from the Canary Islands; a sculpture of the Virgin Mary dating from Fernández de Lugo's time; the Capilla (chapel) de Carta, with artistic wooden carvings; the cross that Fernández de Lugo set up on the site of his first camp when he and his men arrived on the island; and the banners captured from the English squadron led by Nelson that attempted to take Tenerife at the end of the 18th century.

## SAN FRANCISCO CHURCH

This church displays an artistic baroque portico with Solomonic columns. Several interesting altars are retained in the interior. The most valuable pieces are an image of *S Peter of Alcántara* and another depicting *The Sufferings of Christ.*

## THE ISLAND MUSEUM

The 'Museo Insular,' installed on the third floor of the 'Palacio Insular,' is considered to be the most important Archaeology Museum on the Canary Islands. Its stocks include collections of Guanche skulls, primitive weapons and tools, and a reconstruction of a Guanche grave.

## MUNICIPAL MUSEUM

The 'Museo Municipal' houses interesting collections of painting, sculpture and natural sciences. Side by side with canvases by the best artists of the Canary Islands, there are works by Ribera,

**GENERAL VIEW OF GARACHICO.**

Madrazo and other well-known painters from mainland Spain. This building — which accommodates the Municipal Library and Newspaper Library on the ground floor — was the seat of the Law Courts of the Province and, earlier, until the disentailment of the clergy's property promulgated by Mendizábal, it housed a Franciscan monastery of S Peter of Alcántara. Two chapels of this old monastery survive to this day: the aforementioned parish church of

San Francisco and a chapel founded by Irish Catholics who fled from religious persecution in the reign of Queen Elizabeth I of England and took refuge in Tenerife.

## PASO ALTO CASTLE

This castle stands as testimony to the honour of the Canary Islanders who defended Santa Cruz de Tenerife heroically against the attacks of Nelson's squadron on July 25th 1797. The Museum here displays the cannon called 'Tigre,' which fired the shot that destroyed the famous British seaman's arm.

## PALACIO DE CARTA

This mansion, built in the 18th century, stands in Plaza de la Candelaria. It displays an elegant façade of stonework and a typically Canary courtyard and has been classified as a National Monument.

## MONUMENT TO NUESTRA SEÑORA DE CANDELARIA

The monument to Our Lady of Candlemas, in the square of the same name, depicts the Guanches venerating the patron saint of the Canary Islands. This large statue was carved of Carrara marble by the famous Italian sculptor, Antonio Canova, in 1778.

## THE ANAGA ITINERARY

From Plaza de España, in the very centre of Santa Cruz, one can take Avenida de Anaga, leading to several singularly interesting, extreme-

**A TYPICAL HOUSE IN THE VALLE GUERRA.**

ly beautiful parts of the city. From the avenue itself one can enjoy an admirable broad panorama of the bay, with a number of busy terraces giving onto it. In the summer this is one of the places in the city most densely frequented by tourists, especially from nightfall to the early hours of the morning.

Almeida barracks are very near here, as are also the ruins of Paso Alto castle, a fortified bastion dominating the Atlantic which played an important part in the defence of Santa Cruz against Nelson's attacks.

Continuing the itinerary, after passing the Spa the visitor will reach Valleseco, a district of highly distinctive personality, with streets

◁ **OVERALL VIEW OF MASCA.**

THE IMAGE OF THE VIRGIN OF CANDELARIA IS VENERATED IN THIS CHURCH.

INTERIOR OF ONE OF VALLE GUERRA'S TYPICAL HOUSES.

IMAGE OF THE
VIRGIN OF
CANDELARIA, BY
THE SCULPTOR
FERNANDO
ESTÉVEZ.

climbing ramps and steep stairways. The next sight is the picturesque San Andrés fishermen's quarter, still retaining the remains of
the castle of the same name. In San Andrés one can enjoy a spectacle that is always attractive: the fishing boats, patronised by in-
termediaries who come here to buy fish directly on the shores of the
sea. The vast, sandy expanse of Las Teresitas beach begins here.

The road forks at San Andrés. One branch follows the coastline,
featuring enchanting views of the cliffs as it climbs towards Igueste
de San Andrés, where the road ends. The landscapes of this area are
very beautiful: there is luxuriant vegetation and the white walls of a
charming cemetery form a chromatic harmony with the melancholy
green profiles of the cypresses. The rock faces close to the sea,
scaled by cypress-trees in precarious equilibrium, conserve remains
of the Guanches' primitive culture, such as megalithic monuments
and strange stone circles. Beyond, these rugged rocks give way to
the sands of Antequera beach, a splendid inlet that cannot be
reached by land.

The other road branching off from the fork at San Andrés climbs inland, perpendicular to the coast: after passing a series of pronounced zigzags, it leads to El Bailadero, an unusual spot con-
stituting a pass between the mountains. Legend has it that witches
used to meet at El Bailadero to celebrate their sabbaths. Nowadays
the witches seem to have left the area: there are a number of
hostelries at El Bailadero where the visitor can enjoy an excellent dish
of kid, tasty wild rabbit, or some good pork chops.

Three roads lead away from El Bailadero. One crosses the woodland
in which the Cumbres de Anaga National Park has been established.
Another leads — via a long, recently constructed tunnel — down to
the beautiful Taganana valley, one of the most fascinating, picturesque parts of the island. Excellent wines are produced in this valley.
The view of the *magos'* (country people's) houses, scattered irregu-

**SAN MIGUEL CASTLE.**

larly around the cultivated land, is a pleasant one. Until the construction and entry into service of the tunnel mentioned above, Taganana was a legendary spot that could only be reached by sea. The inhabitants of this valley live by agriculture, and also by fishing.

A little distance away from Taganana there is a small fishermen's quarter, near San Roque beach, by the side of which stands a colossal crag. Tachero beach, towards the left, and Almáciga beach, to the right, are also nearby. The little hermitage of the 'Virgen de la Begoña' gives onto the latter beach. The appearance of this image on the coast of Taganana in the 17th century has given rise to various historical hypotheses referring to the presence of the Basques on the island.

The third road leaving El Bailadero constitutes the prolongation of the road from San Andrés. It climbs up to Monte de las Mercedes, becoming narrower as it rises. Not far from Pico del Inglés ('Englishman's Peak') there is a strategically-located natural vantage point from which one can dominate superb broad panoramas stretching over the itineraries already described and reaching as far as the coastline of Santa Cruz, the fertile plain at La Laguna, and the peak of Teide. Cruz del Carmen stands in the centre of Monte de las Mercedes, surmounted by a hermitage with a small square and a vantage point by its side. The surrounding area is embellished by the esplanades called Llano de los Viejos and Llano de los Loros.

## TOUR OF THE NORTH

The recently-built motorway leads from the capital of the island to La Laguna, some 10 km away. If one takes the old main road, however, one will come upon the district of La Laguna called La Cuesta, half-way between the two cities: this is where the main night life establishments are located. Shortly before arriving at La Cuesta, the visitor will find Bella Vista vantage point, dominating splendid panoramas of the city of Santa Cruz.

The quarter called Gracia is a little further on, with its hermitage which was built in 1515. The first meeting of Guanches and conquistadores took place in the interior of this old church dating from

VIEW OF EL MÉDANO BEACH.

the Adelantado Fernández de Lugo's time; no agreement was reached. The stone cross known as the Humilladero (Calvary) stands not
far away, commemorating the conquistadores' victory over the
Guanches on this site. The Humilladero cross marks the municipal
boundary of the city of La Laguna.

# LA LAGUNA

This, the oldest city on Tenerife, is located in the Aguere valley. La Laguna is surrounded by beautiful, highly fertile countryside. The importance of the city's rôle in history is reflected in its wealth of monuments.

The streets of La Laguna are laid out like a grid. The old town is dotted with evocative houses hundreds of years old displaying ancient façades, stone coats of arms, balconies in the style typical of the Canary Islands, and panelled doors. The centre of the old town is Plaza del Adelantado, where Calle de la Carrera and Calle del Agua converge. In this area one can visit the Palacio de Nava, built at the time of the Conquest, and the 18th-century building that was formerly the seat of the Island Council and now houses the City Hall.

# THE CATHEDRAL

The Bishopric of Tenerife was created in 1818 with its see in La Laguna, and the church of Nuestra Señora de los Remedios was raised to the rank of cathedral; in 1897 it was declared to be in ruinous condition, and closed. The cathedral see was then established in San Agustín church, until September 6th 1913, when the present-day cathedral church was consecrated as such. It stands on the former site of Los Remedios church and was built in accordance with plans by José Rodrigo Vallabriga.

The cathedral's interior is characterised by its harmony of form, with the columns, arches and vaults in perfectly balanced proportion to the ensemble. Special mention should be made of the artistic apse and the elegant presbytery, in the neo-Gothic style, which is pre-

THE PALM-TREES RAISE IN STATELY MAJESTY.

ceded by four marble steps. The neo-classical lower choir constitutes a notable work of art.

The most interesting pieces inside La Laguna cathedral include an 18th-century silver processional monstrance, a small crucifix carved by Domingo Estévez, a 16th-century image of the *Virgen de la Luz,* the magnificent organ (built in London in the mid-19th century), the metal screen known as "La Valla," the tabernacle in the chancel (by

Luján Pérez, the great sculptor from the Canary Islands), the tomb of Governor Alonso Fernández de Lugo, whose remains have been buried here since 1881, Bishop Rey Redondo's tomb, and the baroque altarpiece in Los Remedios chapel.

## LA CONCEPCION CHURCH

This is the oldest church on the island: its construction dates from the period of the Conquest, although it was subsequently restored on more than one occasion. The church of Nuestra Señora de la Concepción was classified as a National Monument in 1948. The interior retains an image of the Madonna, carved by Luján Pérez, a fine panel depicting the Evangelist S John (which, according to tradition, "sweated miraculously" in the 17th century), the delicately worked pulpit, artistic coffered ceilings in the nave and choir, and several paintings and sculptures.

## EL CRISTO CHURCH

The church of Christ stands in Plaza de San Francisco; an image of the 'Santísimo Cristo' ('Most Holy Christ') of La Laguna inspiring great popular fervour is venerated inside. The traditional devotion to this figure had its origin in a Gothic carving, acquired at the time of the Adelantado Fernández de Lugo, which was destroyed in 1810 in a fire that devastated the Franciscan monastery where it was kept. This old image of Christ was replaced by the present-day one, which was installed in one of the aisles of the church that survived the fire.

THE UBIQUITOUS PALM-TREES SEEN AGAINST THE LIGHT.

A very popular festivity in honour of the 'Santísimo Cristo' of La Laguna is celebrated in the city on September 14th each year, gathering a multitude of pilgrims from all over the island in the vicinity of Plaza de San Francisco.

VIEW OF THE COSTA DEL SILENCIO.

## OTHER CHURCHES IN LA LAGUNA

Other very interesting churches include Santo Domingo, conserving a number of excellent paintings and sculptures in its interior; Santa Clara Convent, the oldest monastery of all those established on the Canaries, founded by a group of Andalusian nuns who disembarked on the island in the year 1547; the Sanctuary of San Diego del Monte, founded in 1648; San Benito hermitage, dating from 1532, with the image of S Benedict the Abbot in the interior; and the churches of San Lázaro and San Juan Bautista (S John the Baptist).

**LAS GALLETAS, TEMBEL HOUSING DEVELOPMENT ESTATE, ON THE COSTA DEL SILENCIO.**

# SAN FERNANDO UNIVERSITY

The University is situated at the entrance to La Laguna; the campus extends over a spacious esplanade. It is surrounded by residential colleges near Calle de Heraclio Sánchez and Avenida de la Trinidad: these two avenues, and the nearby San Honorato quarter, feature the students' distinctive ambience.

Some of the other important cultural centres at La Laguna are the Instituto de Estudios Canarios, founded in 1933, whose important research programmes are essentially concentrated on subjects related to the culture of the Islands; the Ateneo (Athenaeum), which was created in 1904 and has always displayed laudable intellectual independence; and the Real Sociedad Económica de Amigos del País, dating back to 1777, which has an enlightened encyclopaedist tradition comparable with the atmosphere that shaped similar centres in mainland Spain in the 19th century.

# LA LAGUNA PLAIN

From Plaza de San Francisco there is a road leading to Monte de las Mercedes. This is an absolutely enchanting excursion: not only can the visitor enjoy incomparably beautiful views, but there are also many inns and hostelries the length of the itinerary, offering the typical dishes of the region at very reasonable prices.

The road forks at Las Canteras: the left-hand fork descends via Tegueste and Tejina to Bajamar. This rugged part of Tenerife's coastline is an area of great attraction for tourists. There are three natural swimming-pools and numerous bars and cafés; a Yacht Club was even established here not long ago.

The road comes to an end a few kilometres beyond Punta del Hidalgo. This picturesque fishing village, a singularly attractive spot for tourism, marks the municipal boundary of La Laguna.

THE GOMERA FERRY MOORED IN LOS CRISTIANOS.

DETAIL OF LOS CRISTIANOS.

## TACORONTE

The northern motorway leads from La Laguna to Los Rodeos airport. A little further along is Tacoronte, a town whose district produces famous wines and retains some Guanche caves. The Sanctuary of Christ of Tacoronte stands on the same site as the former San Sebastián hermitage, dating from 1599. The *Cristo de los Dolores* at

Tacoronte is a polychrome carving in the Seville school, a copy of the image sculpted by Domingo de Rioja in the 17th century in accordance with a famous engraving by Dürer.

After passing through the picturesque township of El Sauzal (the site of the celebrated 'Cueva de los Viejos,' a Guanche dwelling located in a cave of the cliff), the visitor will arrive at La Matanza, where the Spanish conquistadores were severely defeated by the Guanches in the course of their attempts to conquer the island.

**DETAIL OF THE BEACH OF LOS CRISTIANOS.**

DETAIL OF THE BEACH OF LAS AMÉRICAS.

## LA OROTAVA VALLEY

This highly fertile, extraordinarily beautiful valley measures some 10 km in breadth, with a surface area of approximately 60 sq.km. Humboldt was amazed by its extension and by the luxuriant vegetation here. The townships of La Orotava, Puerto de la Cruz and Los Reale-

ANOTHER VIEW OF THE BEACH OF LAS AMÉRICAS.

jos are located in La Orotava valley. The splendid Botanical Gardens
(or Acclimatisation Gardens) are at the place known as Durazno, not
far from Puerto de la Cruz: they were established in the late 18th century so as to make it possible to acclimatise on the island various botanical species from America which had not been able to survive in
the gardens at Madrid and Aranjuez.

# LA OROTAVA

This fascinating township bearing the same name as the valley where it lies is surrounded by an immense extension of beautiful flora. Plaza de la Constitución may be said to be the centre of the town; San Juan church, standing at a corner of this square, was built on the site of an earlier hermitage in the middle of the 18th century. The interior of this church retains figures of the *Virgen del Carmen* and the *Virgen de la Gloria,* both carved by Luján Pérez, and also an image of *Christ bound to the Column,* the work of Roldán.

The artistic church of La Concepción, built in 1768, is also very interesting; it has been classified as a historic and artistic monument. The beautiful façade, flanked by a pair of towers, is in the baroque style and displays a superb continuous row of balconies. The outstanding sights in the interior of La Concepción church include the high altar of marble and alabaster, a magnificent Gothic monstrance made of gilt silver, images of the *Madonna, S John* and *S Mary Magdalen* by Luján Pérez, and a depiction of *S Peter* by Rodríguez de la Oliva.

Mention should also be made of the Calvario hermitage, the interior conserving a *Pietà* sculpted by Estévez.

There are brilliant folklore celebrations in the town of La Orotava in the course of the *romería* or pilgrimage of San Isidro; whereas on the day of the Corpus Christi festivity the streets through which the procession passes are literally covered with multicoloured carpets of flowers.

From La Orotava one can undertake interesting excursions to Cruz del Teide, Bosque (Woods) de Aguamansa, El Ancón beach and La Perdoma.

# PUERTO DE LA CRUZ

Nowadays an important centre for international tourism, Puerto de la Cruz is also a city with a distinguished historical past: in the early 18th century it became the real trading capital of the north of the island. The ships bearing the esteemed wines of Tenerife and the island's delicious fruit set sail from Puerto de la Cruz for various foreign countries.

Only traces of the city's original lay-out have survived to the present day, such as the church of Nuestra Señora de la Peña de Francia — built in the 17th century on the site of an earlier hermitage with the same name — and San Telmo church. Plaza del Charco, once the centre of Puerto de la Cruz, has not lost its traditional atmosphere, however; nor has the picturesque fishermen's quarter of La Ranilla. The massive old castle of San Felipe (17th century), formerly a military fortress, stands near La Ranilla; it has been restored and is now a luxurious restaurant.

Nowadays Avenida de Colón ('Columbus Avenue') is effectively the centre of the city: it runs parallel to the sea and stretches as far as the major shopping area at Calle de San Telmo. It is a modern street, with comfortable hotels and bustling cafés. On one side of this cosmopolitan avenue there is a park stretching as far as the coast, with an area of several square kilometres, featuring leafy woodlands, gardens, volcanic rocks, swimming-pools and bars; a modern underground night club has been installed in the centre of the park. The night life of Puerto de la Cruz is very active. There are numerous night clubs and Taoro Casino was opened for gambling not long ago.

SUNSET OVER THE BEACH OF LAS AMÉRICAS.

## LOS REALEJOS

This village, made up of the hamlets of Realejo Alto and Realejo Bajo, was the last refuge of the Guanches in their struggle against the Spanish conquistadores. One of the oldest churches on the island, built by order of Fernández de Lugo, stands in Realejo Alto. Socorro and El Castro beaches are in Realejo Bajo.

El Toscal quarter is in the municipal district of Los Realejos, some 4 km away from the village: there are numerous bars here, where night life continues until dawn.

The enchanting village of San Juan de la Rambla, its little white houses topped by red roofs, is located near Los Realejos.

## ICOD DE LOS VINOS

Icod de los Vinos, a township founded in the year 1501, 38 km away from Puerto de la Cruz, is enclosed by one of the most fascinating landscapes on the whole island. There are numerous aristocratic houses in this town, and many gardens with a profusion of tropical plants. The extensive San Lorenzo de Cáceres park is in the town centre. The most significant monument is San Marcos church, built in successive stages between the 15th and 17th centuries: a stonework building displaying an artistic façade in the Renaissance style. The most remarkable sights in its interior are a large baroque reredos and a valuable image of *S Diego of Alcalá* carved by Pedro de Mena.

The Franciscan monastery (where the image of the *Cristo de las Aguas* is kept) and San Agustín monastery are two other interesting visits. There is an abundance of vineyards, pine-trees, Indian laurels and rock-roses in the vicinity of Icod de los Vinos. The most illustrious floral species, however, is the thousand-year-old dragon-tree, located in San Lorenzo de Cáceres park.

## GARACHICO

Garachico, situated near Icod de los Vinos, was once the most im-

**PUERTO SANTIAGO. LOS GIGANTES CLIFFS.**

portant trading port in the north of Tenerife; in 1706, however, a volcanic eruption of Teide destroyed the town and since then Puerto de la Cruz has been the leading port in the export of fruit. Nowadays Garachico is an attractive seaside town still conserving traces of its past splendour, in particular the old mansions that survived destruction by the lava of the volcano — for example the one that belonged to the Counts of Gomera. Santa Ana is an interesting church here: it was restored in the 18th century, but some remains of the original fabric (early 16th century) survive. San Miguel castle, an old military fortress, stands opposite the bay; it now houses the collections of a museum. One can enjoy views of the impressive rocky massif of the 'Roque de Garachico' from here.

Beyond Garachico the visitor will come upon Buenavista, a village founded in the early 16th century; the church here contains a figure of S Francis by Alonso Cano, valuable altarpieces, and artistic Mudejar coffered ceilings. The municipal area of Buenavista extends over a rugged area of crags and includes the massif of Punta (Headland) de Teno, which can be climbed via Teno de Arriba, through El Palmar valley; subsequently descending via Teno de Abajo, where the lighthouse stands on a volcanic cone. One can also initiate the climb at El Rincón, although this is a more arduous route, or follow the coast via Punta de Teno.

## TOUR OF THE SOUTH

A motorway has now been opened, running almost along the shores of the ocean, and affording access to a number of tourist centres that have sprung up in recent years. The villages and towns along this route generally feature a characteristic structure with an urban area on the inland side, towards the mountains, and a fishing quarter nestling by the seashore.

## CANDELARIA

This picturesque fishing village, lying some 20 km away from Santa

**VIEW OF LOS GIGANTES IN PUERTO SANTIAGO.**

Cruz, is made up of whitewashed houses arranged in terraces around a spacious square giving onto the beach. Candelaria conserves the oldest tradition of devotion to the Virgin Mary on all the Canary Islands.

The throne of the *Virgen Morena,* patron saint of the Archipelago, stands on the beach at Candelaria. Legend has it that this image was found by the Guanches in a nearby ravine in the time of King Damarmo, long before the Conquest. The figure, which appeared at the end of the 14th century, was transferred to the island of Fuerteventura in 1464, but later — as a result of a plague attributed to this act of impiety by the natives — it was returned to Tenerife. In 1826 the image, and a large part of the church sheltering it, were destroyed; it was replaced by a copy, the one now kept in the Basilica standing by the old church. The ancient hermitage where the cultus of the *Virgen de la Candelaria* was initiated still stands, at a corner of the beach. The festivities of the Blessed Virgin Mary are celebrated on August 14th and 15th: on the evening of the 14th, the beach is invaded by a multitude of pilgrims flocking from all over the island of Tenerife. Whole families sleep on the sand, waiting to worship Our Lady of Candlemas the following day. They eat and drink in the open air, under the moonlight, and the songs and strumming of guitars transform the beach into an extraordinary scene, impregnated with folklore.

## ARAFO

This village is near Candelaria; excellent wines are grown in the district. The little inlet called Playa de la Viuda, with black sand, is particularly interesting. Among the rocks are many natural caves that the inhabitants of Arafo have converted into summer homes.

## GÜIMAR

Güimar, lying in the valley of the same name, is the largest town in

**TELEPHERIC TO THE TOP OF EL TEIDE.**

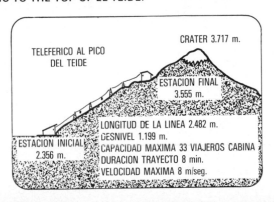

TELEFERICO AL PICO
DEL TEIDE

CRATER 3.717 m.

ESTACION FINAL
3.555 m.

LONGITUD DE LA LINEA 2.482 m.
DESNIVEL 1.199 m.
CAPACIDAD MAXIMA 33 VIAJEROS CABINA
DURACION TRAYECTO 8 min.
VELOCIDAD MAXIMA 8 m/seg.

ESTACION INICIAL
2.356 m.

the southern part of Tenerife. The surrounding district is very fertile, its landscapes fascinatingly colourful. The structure of the town hinges around the 16th-century church of San Pedro Apóstol, which divides the municipality into the quarters known as San Pedro de Arriba and San Pedro de Abajo.

The valley of Güimar is opposite that of La Orotava, on the other side of Tenerife's central cordillera. From Güimar interesting excursions

DETAIL OF A VOLCANIC FORMATION.

can be undertaken to El Puertito (a picturesque summer resort), Arico, Granadilla de Abona, Arona, Los Cristianos, Guía de Isora, Santiago del Teide, El Médano and other places in the south of the island. Splendid views of the valley sloping down towards the sea may be enjoyed from the Mirador (Vantage Point) de Don Martín.

## COSTA DEL SILENCIO

The inauguration of "Reina Sofía" international airport gave great impetus to the development of tourism. The beaches quite close to the airport include Las Batatas, used mainly by nudists, some 5 km from El Médano. Near El Médano there is a small cave that has been converted into a sanctuary: the hermit Pedro de Bethencourt, who founded the Bethlehemite religious order in Guatemala, lived in the cave in the 17th century.

Numerous developments for tourism have grown up in the district of Las Galletas, at the beginning of the extensive "Coast of Silence." The former fishing village of Los Cristianos, a few kilometres away in the municipal district of Arona, has become an important tourist centre in a very short space of time. Diverse facilities have been established facing the little bay here; a quay has even been built, making it possible to link this part of Tenerife with the island of Gomera by means of ferries. There are also a large number of cafés, bars, restaurants, discothèques, apartments and hotels. Nearby Playa de las Américas has become one of the busiest beaches on the Costa del Silencio. Other great tourist attractions on this coast include "Callao Salvaje" and the sandy inlets, which gradually give way to rocky massifs as one approaches Acantilado de los Gigantes ("Giants' Cliff"), at the foot of which a luxury hotel has been built.

**THE AROMATIC BROOM BLOSSOM.**

There is a succession of enchanting hill villages inland, for example Guía de Isora. El Tanque is in this vicinity: a vantage point dominating an extensive, varied panorama in which cultivated land alternates with lava fields, with the sea as a backdrop. Barranco del Infierno ("Hell Ravine"), near Adeje, is enclosed by an imposingly beautiful landscape.

The coastline features the attractions of a series of small fishing villages, such as San Juan, Alcalá or Playa Santiago, their appearance a delight to the eye. After passing the beautiful Caleta (Cove) de Adeje, the visitor will come upon Tamaimo and Santiago Valley with Santiago del Teide in the centre, surrounded by vineyards and fields sown with cereals. This is the edge of the arid, rocky, desert area. From Arguallo or Tamaimo one can undertake an interesting excursion to El Chinyero volcano and Valle de Masca. Cruz de Erjos, finally, gives onto the landscapes of the northern part of Tenerife: very fertile lands, boasting a wealth of colour, extending downwards on either side of a road that descends towards Garachico on the coast.

## ITINERARY OF THE CENTRAL MOUNTAINS

This route commences in the outskirts of La Laguna, at the Glorieta del Brasil, and leads up towards Monte de La Esperanza. After a few kilometres the visitor will reach the Safari Park, where elephants, leopards, hippopotami, giraffes, monkeys, zebus and ostriches live side by side with other zoological species.

The slopes of Monte de La Esperanza are scattered with inns and taverns here and there, where the diverse specialities of Canary Islands cuisine are served. As one advances towards the summit of the mountain, the vegetation becomes thicker. Once past the altitude of 2,000 metres, the landscape offered to one's eyes features an extraordinary wealth of colours. El Diablillo vantage point dominates a marvellous panorama of La Orotava valley.

**THE SUMMIT OF EL TEIDE SEEN FROM LAS CAÑADAS.**

# EL PORTILLO

When one arrives at this large relatively level area, the landscape suddenly changes in nature. Lands of volcanic structure make their appearance and the landscape resembles the surface of the moon, as a result of the strange forms configured over the passage of time by the lava from the eruptions of Teide, which is near this zone.

Despite its characteristically lunar landscapes, the area offers great attractions for tourism; there are restaurants and bars on all sides. El Portillo is almost permanently occupied by wave upon wave of tourists, who arrive from different parts of the island in coaches.

A steep, zigzagging road leads down from El Portillo towards La Orotava, affording incomparably beautiful panoramas. All the colourful splendour of La Orotava valley stretches out before one's eyes, with the blue waters of the Atlantic forming an insuperable chromatic counterpoint in the distance.

La Caldera is approximately 10 km from El Portillo. This is a vast esplanade containing a pleasant recreational park which is used as a stopping place by many visitors, for — apart from all the necessary installations for children to play — there are also benches, tables and fireplaces at the disposal of those who wish to eat while they rest.

## LAS CAÑADAS

Las Cañadas ("The Ravines") National Park comprises a gigantic level area at the foot of Teide. To reach the Park one should set out from Santa Cruz and, once past the outskirts of La Laguna, take the road following the central mountains up towards Monte de La Esperanza. From the point known as El Diablillo, at kilometre stone number 20, 1,500 metres above sea-level, one can descry both the north and south sides of the island and enjoy splendid panoramas stretching towards the horizon. The visitor must then cross the northern side of Chirijer mountain. As one continues climbing, the valleys of Güimar, on the southern coast, and La Orotava — on the northern side — appear before one's eyes.

LAS CAÑADAS. THE VOLCANIC GEOLOGY OF THE ISLAND PRODUCES
EXAMPLES AS CURIOUS AS THIS STONE ROSE.

Many spots should be admired in this area, in particular the Articosia zone, El Dique del Abuelo, Chipeque Mountain, the Fuente ('Fountain') de Joco, Roque (Rock) de Acele, Arafo Volcano, Degollada de la Crucita and Collado (Pass) de Izaña. From the junction at Collado de Izaña there is a ramp leading to the Observatory of the same name — which is at an altitude of 2,362 metres above sea-level, 53 km from the capital of the island — and to the Spanish Television relay station. The itinerary continues from here towards El Portillo de la Villa, entering the area of Las Cañadas properly speaking, and then Montaña Blanca, the starting point for the climb to the summit of Teide. The route from Montaña Blanca to Boca de Tauce passes through Cañada Blanca, Los Bosques vantage point, Los Azulejos and Llano (Plain) de Ucanca. This route enables the traveller to admire a landscape of impressive beauty, with the Ucanca valley stretching out below the road. There are strangely-shaped blocks of stone that keep their balance as if by sheer miracle, and the rugged crests of Los Roques are outlined in the background. This striking landscape constitutes a really impressive spectacle of Nature.

The Parador Nacional (luxury State hotel) is near the vantage point giving onto the Ucanca Plain, by the side of the hermitage devoted to the Virgen de las Nieves. The structure of the Parador is similar to that of a mountain refuge, with stone walls, wooden floors, sturdy shutters and solid beams. The hotel has a swimming-pool considered to be the one located at the greatest altitude of all those in Spain; and is sometimes cut off by snow in winter.

Two roads link the wild, majestic area of Boca de Tauce with the rest of the island. One of them leads into the striking, beautiful sea of black stone called *Malpaís,* also known as Valle de la Santidad. The road begins to descend sharply at the end of this majestic volcanic

**CATACEA OF THE GENUS OPUNTIA, A VERY ABUNDANT SPECIES IN THE SOUTH OF THE ISLAND.**

desert, and leads down to Tamaimo through the verdure of thick woodlands.

The other road from Boca de Tauce descends in the opposite direction from the one just described. Its route, constantly zigzagging, enables one to contemplate splendid panoramas of the abyss below, embellished by the enchanting fronds of the woods. This road passes through the little village of Vilaflor, the highest one on the whole island. Vilaflor is famous for its delicious goats' milk cheeses, and also because Pedro de Bethencourt was born there — he was baptised in San Pedro church, built in the 16th century. The same road leads to Granadilla, an important agricultural centre on the south side of the island, lying in a fertile district where the best oranges in Tenerife are grown. The magnificent beach of El Médano is 11 km away: the island's paradise for international tourism begins here.

## TEIDE

The mythical peak of Teide — proud of its superiority, with all the im-

CAMEL RIDES ARE JUST ONE OF THE TOURIST ATTRACTIONS IN PUERTO DE LA CRUZ.

**CAMEL-TAXIS AWAITING A FARE**.

pressive majesty of a Cyclops with ancient Greek ancestry — stands over the colossal cirque of Las Cañadas. Teide's crater measures 12 km in diameter, 75 km in circumference. The eruptions of the volcano have left their mark on the surrounding lands, with colours ranging from white through blue, red and yellow to black. Everything in and around Teide appears fantastic, as if shrouded in a veil of legend; Herodotus called the volcano "a column in the sky," and it

A CARPET CREATED WITH COLOURED EARTH, COVERING THE PLAZA DEL AYUNTAMIENTO IN LA OROTAVA DURING THE FESTIVALS OF CORPUS CHRISTI.

THE GAY
ARTISAN-WORK
OF LA OROTAVA.

**THE POPULAR MUSIC FROM GOMERA IS NOT ONLY SUNG BUT ALSO WHISTLED.**

constitutes an inexhaustible source of legends vying with one another in their fantasticalness.

Teide's summit is the highest in all Spain, with an altitude of 3,716 metres above sea-level. It is surrounded by imposing massifs of cleft rocks, like monstrous fruits shrivelled by infernal fire, and mountains of pumice-stone. According to geologists, when Las Cañadas collapsed, Teide would belch forth fire, clouds of dismal smoke, devastating winds and burning sand.

The towering height of Teide soars above a retinue of other peaks, practically dwarfed by the fabulous summit, such as El Cabezón, La Fortaleza, El Sombrero de Chasna, El Topo de la Grieta or Guajara, all of which are over 2,000 m high.

The ascent of Teide starts from Montaña Blanca, near Las Cañadas, with at its feet the terminal of the cableway leading to the vicinity of the gigantic crater. To reach the crater itself one must then walk a short distance, but this is a laborious climb taking at least twenty minutes, as a result not only of the shortage of oxygen characteristic

**TOBACCO PROCESSING, TRANSFORMING THE PLANT INTO CIGARS.**

TWO VIEWS OF
THE TENERIFE
CARNIVAL,
RECALLING ITS
TROPICAL
ORIGINS.

**LORO PARQUE INSTALLATIONS.**

of such altitudes, but also of the effects of the fumaroles and sulphurous smoke given off by the volcano. The vicinity of La Rambleta and Las Narices del Teide ("Teide's Nostrils") is particularly contaminated: the fumaroles emitting sulphurous fumes are more intense here. The view from the summit of Teide is grandiose: the outlines of the islands of Gomera, Hierro, La Palma and even Gran Canaria seem to cluster humbly around the feet of the volcano.

PARROTS ARE AN ESSENTIAL ELEMENT IN THE TROPICAL COLOUR OF
PUERTO DE LA CRUZ.

Everything is dwarfed by the majesty of Teide, prostrate below its peak; only the firmament seems to sustain the gaze of the volcano. It is as if Teide, like some arrogant pagan god, wished to set itself up as the supreme lord of both Nature and mankind. People admire it when they view it from the land, and are struck with astonishment when they descry it from the sea. The intrepid mariners of times gone by, who plied the seas in their fragile craft, used to say, "In the Ocean there is a mountain called Atlas, which is conical and so high that one cannot glimpse its summit." This was Teide.

TYPICAL TENERIFE FARE: THE FISH OR «VIEJA», THE «GOFIO», SWEET POTATOES, THE «MOJO»...

# tenerife

Puerto la C

Playa de Sto. Domingo

San Juan de la Rambla
Playa de S. Marcos
La Guancha
Realejo Bajo
Realejo Alto

Caleta Andén

Buenavista del Norte
Los Silos
Garachico
**cod de los Vinos** (Los Realejos)

Pta. de Teno

Portillo de la Villa

Santiago del Teide

Arguay

Teide 3718
Cueva del Hielo

Playa de la Arena

Boca d Piauce

Guía de Isora

Playa de S. Juan

Vilaflor
**Granadilla de Abona**

Adeje

Arona
S. Migu

La Caleta

Playa Las Américas
**Playa Honda**

Cano
Blanco
Aldea Blanca

Los Cristianos

El Abri

**La Arenita**

Las Galletas

**Playa de Confital**

Pta. del Hidalgo

**Playa del Roque**

Pta. de Anaga

**Playa del Arenal**

Taganana

Tejina

Tegueste

Valle de Igueste

**(La Laguna)**
San Cristóbal

S. Andrés

Tacoronte

**Playa de las Teresitas**

Sauzal

aleta de
Negra

Aeropuerto
de los Rodeos

**SANTA CRUZ DE TENERIFE**

Sta.
Ursula

La Matanza
de Acentejo

**Playa de Lomo**

La Victoria
de Acentejo

**Playa de los Naos**

de S. Felipe

**La Orotava**

Igueste

Candelaria

Arafo

Iñaña
2387

Izaña

**Playa de la**

][ Pto. de
Güimar

**Güimar**

**La Caleta**

Fasnia

**Playa de la Margarella**

eva del
de Herque

Los Roques

**Playa de Topuerque**

Arico
El Viejo

ico

Poris de
Bona

Pta. de Abona

**Playa del Medano**

Roja

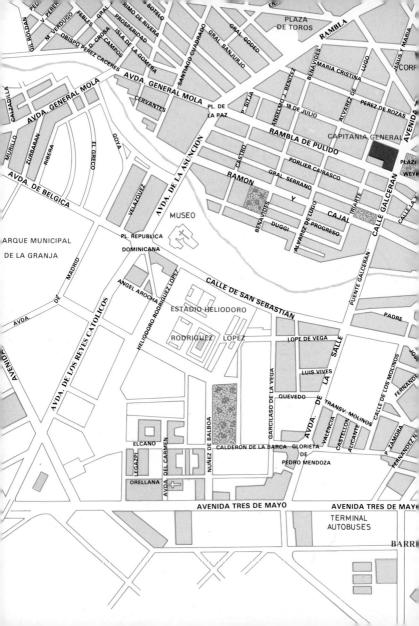

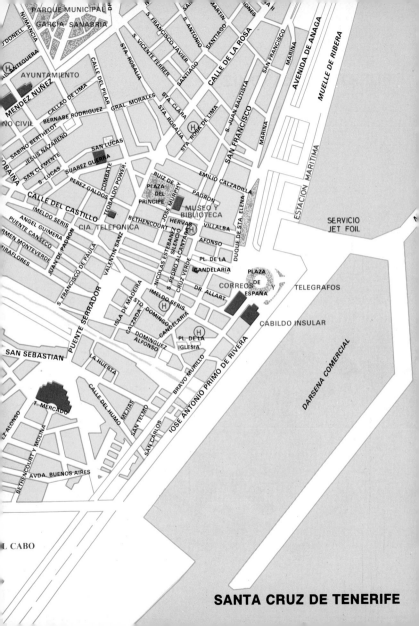

SANTA CRUZ DE TENERIFE

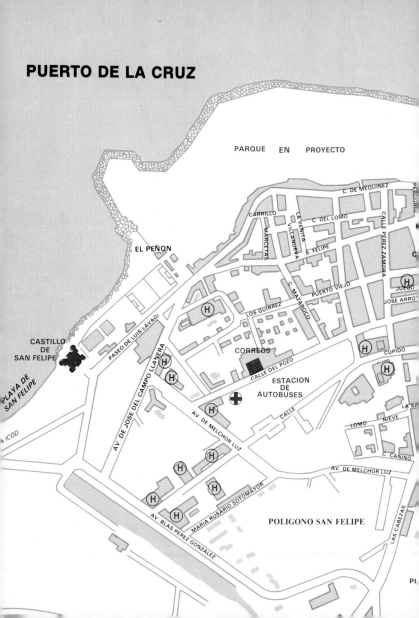

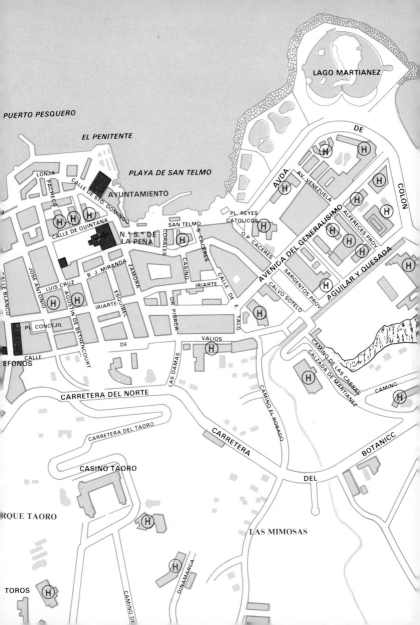

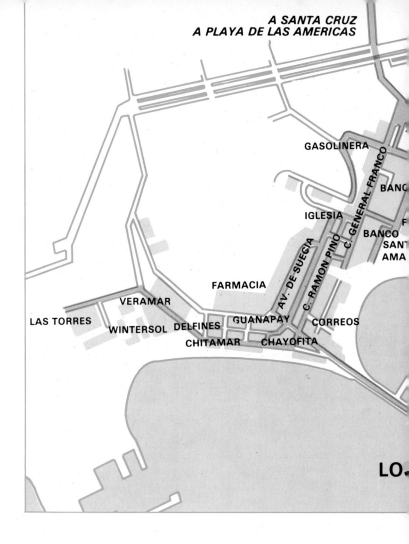

A LAS GALLETAS

LA SIRENA

ATLANTIDA

PRINCESA DACIL

ACAY

SOL

R

GUAYERO

EL CARMEN

CRISTIAN MAR

COMODORO

COSTA MAR

EL PUERTITO

CRISTIANOS

RINCON DE LOS CRISTIANOS

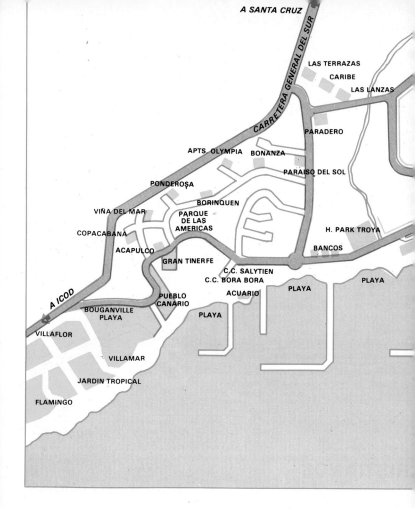

A SANTA CRUZ

CARRETERA GENERAL DEL SUR

LAS TERRAZAS
CARIBE
LAS LANZAS

PARADERO

APTS. OLYMPIA BONANZA

PARAISO DEL SOL

PONDEROSA

BORINQUEN

VIÑA DEL MAR
PARQUE
DE LAS
AMERICAS

COPACABANA

H. PARK TROYA

ACAPULCO

BANCOS

GRAN TINERFE

C.C. SALYTIEN
C.C. BORA BORA

PLAYA

ACUARIO

PLAYA

PUEBLO
CANARIO

A ICOD

BOUGANVILLE
PLAYA

PLAYA

VILLAFLOR

VILLAMAR

JARDIN TROPICAL

FLAMINGO

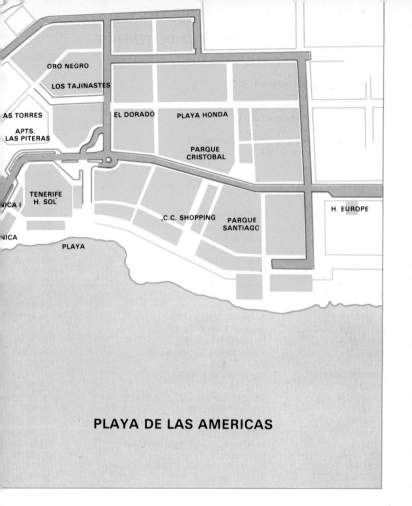

ORO NEGRO

LOS TAJINASTES

AS TORRES

APTS.
LAS PITERAS

EL DORADO          PLAYA HONDA

PARQUE
CRISTOBAL

TENERIFE
H. SOL

NICA I

NICA

PLAYA

C.C. SHOPPING     PARQUE
                  SANTIAGO

H. EUROPE

**PLAYA DE LAS AMERICAS**

# TEMPERATURES IN SANTA CRUZ DE TENERIFE
## (CENTIGRADE)

Absolute maxium temperature: 40°
Absolute minimum temperature: 12°
Average maximum temperature: 24°
Average minimum temperature: 18°
Rainy days per year: 106
Average temperature sea water in summer: 21°
Hours of sun per year: 2,759

## CONSULATES IN SANTA CRUZ DE TENERIFE

| | | |
|---|---|---|
| AUSTRIA | Pl. San Francisco, 17 | 24 37 99 |
| BELGIUM | Pl. San Francisco, 9, 2.° | 24 11 93 |
| BOLIVIA | General Franco, 141 | 28 68 00 |
| BRASIL | Castillo, 54 | 28 65 12 |
| CHILE | Villalba Hervás, 2, 4° | 24 14 90 |
| COLUMBIA | Bethencourt Alfonso, 25, 3° | |
| COSTA RICA | Enrique Wolfson, 13 bajos | 21 75 33 |
| DENMARK | Avda. de Anaga, 43 | 27 57 57 |
| FINLAND | Avda. de Anaga, 43, 2° | 28 09 55 |
| GERMANY | Avda. de Anaga, 43 | 28 48 12 |
| GREAT BRITAIN | Suárez Guerra, 40, 5° | 24 20 00 |
| HONDURAS | Puerta Canseco, 47, 2° | 28 75 69 |
| IRELAND | Avda. Reyes Católicos, 29 | 24 70 46 |
| ITALY | Pilar, 27 2° | 27 57 09 |
| LUXEMBOURG | San Francisco, 9, 2.° | 24 11 93 |
| MONACO | Pilar, 14, 1° | 28 25 50 |
| NETHERLANDS | Edificio Hamilton, 3°, Oficina 35 | 24 35 75 |
| NORWAY | Doctor Zerolo, 14 | 28 73 51 |
| PANAMA | Puerta Canseco, 47 | 28 86 08 |
| PARAGUAY | General Franco, 55 | 27 46 43 |
| PERU | La Marina, 7 - Edificio Hamilton | 24 53 49 |
| PORTUGAL | Velázquez, 11 | 22 69 73 |
| SWEDEN | Av. de Anaga, 43, 1° - Edif. Océano | 27 74 50 |
| UNITED STATES | Alvarez de Lugo, 10 | 28 69 50 |
| URUGUAY | 25 de Julio, 15 | 27 69 65 |
| VENEZUELA | Pilar, 27, 1° | 27 33 16 |

## CONSULATES IN PUERTO DE LA CRUZ

| | | |
|---|---|---|
| GAMBIA | Hotel Loro Parque | 38 30 12 |
| GUINEA BISSAU | Apto. 301 - Edificio Duraflor | 38 12 91 |
| SENEGAL | Apto. 301 - Edificio Duraflor | 38 12 91 |

# CONSULATES IN SANTA CRUZ DE LA PALMA

VENEZUELA                    Odaly, 31                         41 12 19

## USEFUL AND EMERGENY TELEPHONE NUMBERS

| | |
|---|---|
| Canaries Electricity Board - Santa Cruz de Tenerife | 24 18 90 |
| Crane (24-Hour Service) - Santa Cruz de Tenerife | 25 44 29 |
| Cultural Information - Santa Cruz de Tenerife | 28 88 88 |
| Fire Stations: Santa Cruz de Tenerife | 22 00 80 |
| La Laguna | 25 10 80 |
| La Orotava | 33 00 80 |
| Los Realejos | 33 00 80 |
| Puerto de la Cruz | 33 00 80 |
| Santa Cruz de la Palma | 41 11 50 |
| First-Aid Centres: Santa Cruz de Tenerife | 24 15 02 |
| Icod de los Vinos | 81 07 11 |
| La Laguna | 25 87 77 |
| La Orotava | 33 01 01 |
| Los Realejos | 34 05 56 |
| Puerto de la Cruz | 38 38 12 |
| Santa Cruz de la Palma | 41 21 40 |
| First-Aid on the Road - Güimar | 51 08 60 |
| Municipal Police: Santa Cruz de Tenerife | 21 51 00 |
| Icod de los Vinos | 81 06 61 |
| La Laguna | 25 10 80 |
| La Orotava | 33 01 14 |
| Los Realejos | 34 06 00 |
| Puerto de la Cruz | 38 04 28 |
| Santa Cruz de la Palma | 41 11 50 |
| Municipal Water Board - Santa Cruz de Tenerife | 21 27 22 |
| Out-of-Hours Chemists (Information) - Santa Cruz de Tenerife | 28 24 24 |
| Police: Santa Cruz de Tenerife | 091 |
| Icod de los Vinos | 81 11 50 |
| La Laguna | 091 - 25 53 41 |
| La Orotava | 33 29 65 |
| Puerto de la Cruz | 38 12 24 |
| Santa Cruz de la Palma | 41 40 43 |
| Post Office: | |
| Santa Cruz de Tenerife          Plaza de España | 24 20 02 |
| La Laguna          Plaza Santo Domingo | 25 96 05 |
| Puerto de la Cruz          Agustín Bethencourt, 15 | 38 58 05 |
| Santa Cruz de la Palma          Plaza del Muelle, 2 | 41 17 02 |
| Telegrammes by telephone - Santa Cruz de Tenerife | 22 20 00 |
| Telegraphs: Santa Cruz de Tenerife          Plaza de España | 24 13 88 |

| | | |
|---|---|---|
| Puerto de la Cruz | Agustín de Bethencourt, 15 | 38 57 16 |
| Santa Cruz de la Palma | Plaza del Muelle, 2 | 41 11 67 |
| Telephone Companies: Santa Cruz de Tenerife | Unamuno, 4 | 004 |
| La Laguna | | 004 |
| Puerto de la Cruz | | 004 |
| Santa Cruz de la Palma | | 004 |

# AIRPORTS

| | | |
|---|---|---|
| Santa Cruz de Tenerife | Los Rodeos National Airport | 25 79 40 |
| | South Airport (Queen Sofia) | 77 00 50 |
| Isla de Hierro | Valverde | 55 08 79 |
| Santa Cruz de la Palma | | 41 13 45 |

# TOURISM OFFICES

**Santa Cruz de Tenerife:**

| | | |
|---|---|---|
| Information Office | José Antonio, 2 | 24 22 27 |
| Insular Tourism | José Antonio, 2 | 24 20 90 |
| Provincial Delegation | Marina, 57 | 28 21 54 |

**Puerto de la Cruz:**

| | | |
|---|---|---|
| Tourist Office | Plaza de la Iglesia, s/n | 38 43 28 |

# URBAN TRANSPORT

| | | |
|---|---|---|
| Santa Cruz de Tenerife - Information | Avda. Bravo Murillo | 24 30 23 |
| La Laguna - Information | Plaza de San Cristóbal | 25 94 12 |
| La Orotava - Information | Calvario, 42 | 33 27 02 |
| Puerto de la Cruz - Information | Carrero Blanco | 38 18 07 |
| Santa Cruz de la Palma - Information | Quinta, 8 | 41 19 24 |

# TAXI RANKS

| | |
|---|---|
| Santa Cruz de Tenerife - San Marcos | 64 12 09 |
| San Cristóbal | 64 43 17 |
| Santa Cruz | 21 39 33 |
| Tenerife | 61 64 04 |
| Siete Islas | 61 51 90 |
| Autotaxi Provincial Cooperative | 21 20 77 |

| La Laguna - Airport | | 25 87 95 |
|---|---|---|
| Avda. Trinidad, s/n | | 25 85 32 |
| Las Mercedes, 27 | | 25 76 28 |
| Pl. Dr. Oliveras, s/n | | 25 99 04 |
| Pl. de la Catedral, s/n | | 25 99 00 |
| Radio Taxis | | 25 36 77 |
| Santa Cruz de la Palma - Miguel Sosvilla, s/n | | 41 11 07 |
| Puerto de la Cruz - Pl. General Franco s/n | | 38 58 18 |

## CLINICS AND HOSPITALS

**Santa Cruz de Tenerife:**

| | | |
|---|---|---|
| Centro Médico Quirúrgico | Enrique Wolfson, 8 | 27 66 50 |
| | | 28 70 08 |
| Clínica Bencomo | San Lucas, 7, 3º y 4º | 28 41 00 / 04 / 08 |
| Clínica La Colina | Salamanca Chica (Ciudad Jardín) | 27 07 00 |
| | | 28 07 00 |
| Hospital Cabildo Insular | Urbanización Ofra, s/n | 64 10 11 |
| | | 64 54 11 |
| | | 64 63 12 |
| Children' Hospital | | 28 65 50 |

**Puerto de la Cruz:**

| | | |
|---|---|---|
| Clínica Tamaragua | Agustín de Bethencourt, 28 | 38 05 12 |

**La Laguna:**

| | | |
|---|---|---|
| Centro Médico de Urgencias Sanitarias | Avda. Trinidad, 39 | 25 30 35 |
| | | 25 59 53 |
| Hospital Cabildo Insular | Sol Ortega, 11 | 25 95 32 |

**La Orotava:**

| | | |
|---|---|---|
| Sáez Tapia | Urbanización San Miguel | 33 05 50 |

**Icod de los Vinos:**

| | | |
|---|---|---|
| Hospital | San Antonio, 7 | 81 07 86 |

**San Sebastián de la Gomera:**

| | | |
|---|---|---|
| Hospital Insular | Calvario, s/n | 87 04 50 |
| | | 87 09 06 |

**Puerto de la Cruz:**

| | | |
|---|---|---|
| Hospital Puerto de la Cruz | Cologan, s/n | 38 19 58 |

## AIRLINES

| | | |
|---|---|---|
| ALITALIA (Puerto de la Cruz) | Avda. Generalísimo, 25 | 38 40 52 |
| AIR FRANCE | Bethencourt Alfonso, 8 | 24 75 90 |
| AVIACO | Reina Sofía Airport | 77 13 09 |
| | | 77 12 00 |
| | | 77 12 04 |

| IBERIA | Avda. de Anaga, 23 | 28 11 00 |
| | | 28 11 50 |
| LUFTHANSA (Puerto de la Cruz) | Avda. Generalísimo, s/n | 38 55 12 |
| SAS | Doctor Zerolo, 14 | 28 20 62 |
| SPANTAX | Reina Sofía Airport | 77 13 68 |
| STERLING AIRWAYS | Reina Sofía Airport | 77 10 15 |
| VIASA | Bethencourt Alfonso, 10, 3.° | 24 24 75 |
| | | 24 24 76 |

## SHIPPING LINES

| AUCONA | La Marina, 59 | 28 78 50 |
| | | 28 79 00 |
| | | 28 79 50 |
| TRANSMEDITERRANEA | La Marina, 59 | 28 57 61 |
| | | 24 30 12 |
| TRANSATLANTICA ESPAÑOLA | Pilar, 36 | 27 71 58 |

## TRAVEL AGENCIES

| AMERICA | General Sanjurjo, 50 | 28 35 00 |
| ATLANTICA | Bethencourt Alfonso, 18 | 24 59 79 |
| FERNANDO POO | Marina, 11 | 24 20 77 |
| MELIA | Pilar, 9 | 24 63 96 |
| PHILEAS FOGG | 25 de Julio, 4 | 28 12 04 |
| ROSAL | Avda. de Bélgica, 3 | 22 24 45 |
| | | 22 26 45 |
| SOLYMAR | Villalba Hervás, 15 | 24 71 71 |
| | | 24 70 82 |
| WAGONS LITS | Pilar, 2 | 24 66 83 |

## LIBRARIES, CLUBS AND ATHENAEUMS

**Santa Cruz de Tenerife:**
| 12th of January Circle of Friendship | Ruíz Padrón, 8 | 24 66 96 |
| Fine Arts Circle | Castillo, 47 | 24 26 49 |
| Merchantile Circle | Plaza Candelaria, 6 | 24 12 83 |
| Municipal Historical Archives | Comodoro Rolin, s/n | 21 71 44 |
| Municipal Library | José Murphy, 1 | 24 38 08 |
| Music Conservatory | Avda. Asuncionista, s/n | 22 84 04 |
| Royal Automobile Club | Avda. de Anaga | 27 07 16 |
| Royal Pigeon Society | General Fanjul, 17 | 27 19 10 |

| | | |
|---|---|---|
| Royal Sailing Club | Carretera San Andrés | 27 37 00 |
| Seamen's Association | Avda. de Anaga | 27 11 50 |
| Tenerife Casino | Plaza Candelaria | 24 25 90 |
| **La Laguna:** | | |
| Atalaya Riding Club | San Lázaro, Km 11 | 25 14 10 |
| Athenaeum | Pl. de la Catedral, 3 | 25 98 22 |
| Golf Club | Glorieta Peñón, s/n | 25 02 40 |
| Pigeon-shooting Club | Mesa Mota | 25 78 45 |
| **La Orotava:** | | |
| Liceo Taoro Cultural Society | Plaza de la Constitución | 33 01 19 |
| **Los Realejos:** | | |
| El Casino Cultural and | | |
| Recreative Society | General Franco, 3 | 34 07 08 |
| **Puerto de la Cruz:** | | |
| Institute of Hispanic Studies | Quintana, s/n | 38 37 31 |
| **San Sebastián de la Gomera:** | | |
| La Gomera Sailing Club | Cueva del Conde, s/n | 87 10 02 |
| **Santa Cruz de la Palma:** | | |
| Royal Sailing Club | El Roque | 41 10 78 |
| Tennis Club | La Caldereta | 41 10 12 |
| **Valverde:** | | |
| Valverde Casino | Jesús Nazareno, s/n | 55 00 30 |

# Contents

THE GARDEN OF THE
 HESPERIDES                          5
HISTORICAL OUTLINE OF
 THE ISLANDS                        14
TENERIFE                            24
CLIMATE AND FLORA                   32
FOLK CULTURE                        38
SPORTS                              46
CRAFT WORK                          48
CUISINE                             50
TYPICAL CANARY
 ARCHITECTURE                       58
THE CAPITAL OF TENERIFE             60
THE BEACHES OF TENERIFE             60
THE HARBOUR                         62
THE CITY                            64
CHURCH OF NUESTRA SEÑORA
 DE LA CONCEPCION                   79
SAN FRANCISCO CHURCH                80
THE ISLAND MUSEUM                   80
MUNICIPAL MUSEUM                    80
PASO ALTO CASTLE                    82
PALACIO DE CARTA                    82
MONUMENT TO NUESTRA
 SEÑORA DE CANDELARIA               82

THE ANAGA ITINERARY                  8
TOUR OF THE NORTH                    9
LA LAGUNA                            9
THE CATHEDRAL                        9
LA CONCEPCION CHURCH                 9
EL CRISTO CHURCH                     9
OTHER CHURCHES IN
 LA LAGUNA                         10(
SAN FERNANDO UNIVERSITY            10:
LA LAGUNA PLAIN                    102
TACORONTE                         104
LA OROTAVA VALLEY                 106
LA OROTAVA                        108
PUERTO DE LA CRUZ                 110
LOS REALEJOS                      111
ICOD DE LOS VINOS                 112
GARACHICO                         112
TOUR OF THE SOUTH                 114
CANDELARIA                        114
ARAFO                             116
GÜIMAR                            116
LA COSTA DEL SILENCIO             120
ITINERARY OF THE CENTRAL
 MOUNTAINS                        122
EL PORTILLO                       124
LAS CAÑADAS                       126
TEIDE                             130

The printing of this book was completed
in the workshops of FISA - Industrias
Gráficas, Palaudarias, 26 - Barcelona
(Spain)